The Seven Words

S W Webb

Fortheile 1.20

W J Kurtz

July 52

The

Seven Words

CLOVIS G. CHAPPELL

ABINGDON-COKESBURY PRESS

New York • *Nashville*

THE SEVEN WORDS

COPYRIGHT MCMLII
BY PIERCE AND SMITH

SET UP, PRINTED, AND BOUND BY THE PARTHENON PRESS, AT NASHVILLE, TENNESSEE, UNITED STATES OF AMERICA

To

my two brothers, who were ministers,
EDWIN AND ASHLEY
with tender and grateful memories

» »» » » » »

Contents

The First Word

> "*Father, forgive them; for they know not what they do.*"

LUKE 23:34

It is Good Friday, in the year 33 A.D.!

HAD YOU BEEN IN JERUSALEM ON THIS FATEFUL FRIDAY that changed the world, you would doubtless have been brought under the spell of the excitement of the hour. This excitement was born of the fact that three prisoners were about to pay the death penalty. One of them was a prophet from Nazareth. The other two were revolutionists. The crowd, with a natural love of the gruesome, was hideously eager for the show. This eagerness was doubtless heightened by the fact that all three of the doomed men were well known. This was certainly the case with the prophet. It was probably true of the two outlaws as well.

Not only were all three of these men well known, but they were all popular. The two revolutionists were ardent patriots. Having fought like men, like men they were determined to die. The crowd naturally looked upon them as heroes. The prophet had also been popular. He was so still. This was the case in spite of the fact

9

that most of those immediately surrounding the cross were intensely hostile. So bitter was their antagonism that, having nailed Jesus to the cross, they would not allow him to die in peace. Even the revolutionists, caught under the spell of their bitter antagonism, added their own insults to the senseless howls of the mob and to the cruel jibes of the churchmen. Then something took place that at first silenced one of these revolutionists, then changed his insults into prayers. What happened? The man on the central cross prayed this prayer, "Father, forgive them; for they know not what they do."

I

The fact that the first word that Jesus uttered upon his cross was a prayer does not surprise us. His had been a habit of prayer from his youth. Naturally, he would pray in this black and desperate hour. Even those who refuse to pray when the sea of life is smooth generally refuse no longer when their sea is being whipped by a tempest. There is a sense in which prayer is all but instinctive. When the ground gives way beneath our feet, when some dire tragedy wrenches every visible support from our clinging fingers, we reach for the Unseen almost as naturally as we shrink from a blow. But when we pray under such circumstances, it is almost invariably for ourselves. In our need we cry, "Lord, help me." Nor is there anything wrong in such prayers. We are invited to come boldly to the throne of grace that we may obtain mercy and find grace to help in every time of need. Had Jesus, therefore, thus prayed, it would have been only the natural and the expected.

But what does thrill us is that this first word of prayer that Jesus offered was not for himself. He did not ask for his own deliverance. He did not pray in that black hour for his loved ones, nor for his friends. He prayed for his enemies. He prayed for the soldiers and for the far more cruel churchmen who, having nailed him to the cross, were even then howling about him. It was around the bloody shoulders of these murderers that he flung the folds of this prayer, "Father, forgive them; for they know not what they do."

Once on a certain hill Jesus had preached in this fashion, "Ye have heard that it hath been said, Thou shalt love thy neighbour, and hate thine enemy. But I say unto you, Love your enemies, . . . and pray for them which despitefully use you." On another occasion he had commanded his followers to forgive, not once, but "until seventy times seven"—that is, without limit. Forgiveness was to flow from their hearts as constantly as waters from a gushing spring. What he had preached on the sunny hill of the Sermon on the Mount, he practiced on the grim hill of Calvary. Here he is offering unlimited forgiveness.

II

In asking forgiveness for his murderers Jesus was asking the best possible. This is the case because forgiveness means far more than being let off from a penalty. I am

11

thinking now of a man who committed murder. There was no possible doubt as to his guilt. He was tried and was sentenced to pay the penalty for his crime. But it so happened that he was a man of political influence. He had a heavy claim on the governor of his state. Therefore he was no sooner sentenced than he received a pardon. But in spite of his pardon he still had the stain of blood upon his hands. When God pardons, he does something for us that is far better than merely refusing to punish us as we deserve.

No more is forgiveness a way of escape from the consequences of our wrongdoing. If we sow tares, we are going to reap them, even though we find forgiveness. When David in hot blood had been guilty of adultery, when in cold blood he had committed murder, his faithful minister took his life in his hands and rebuked him for his sin. Then what? David might have come to hate his physician rather than his deadly disease. But he chose the wiser course. As Nathan spoke home to his heart, David's knees went weak, and with a voice choked by sobs he clutched at God's skirts and prayed, "Have mercy upon me." His prayer was not in vain. God heard and answered. He gave to the sinner abundant pardon. But though this forgiveness was full and complete, it did not save David from the terrible consequences of his sin. Instead, he suffered in brokenness of heart to the very end of his days.

A few years ago I went to see a woman who was dying of bichloride of mercury self-administered. She told me of the bitter experience through which she had passed. "At last," she declared, "I felt that I could not bear it any longer. But I am sorry now. I realize that I have done wrong. The reason I have sent for you is to ask you this question, Will God forgive me?"

With complete confidence I answered in the affirmative. I offered her salvation in the name of him who "was wounded for our transgressions." She claimed to accept that salvation, and I feel confident she went to meet her Lord in peace. But there was one something that this forgiveness did not do. It did not take the poison from her tortured body. In spite of the fact that she had been fully forgiven, she died.

What, then, is forgiveness? It is the restoration of a fellowship. When God forgives, he takes us back into his friendship and walks with us as if we had never sinned. He forgets all our ugly past. This is his own promise, "I will forgive their iniquity, and I will remember their sin no more." He treats us as Jesus treated his friends who failed him so miserably in Gethsemane. He had leaned heavily upon these friends. But the best they could do was to go to sleep. More than once he came to wake them, but in spite of all his efforts they threw their big chance away. So what? In spite of their failure we hear our Lord saying to them, "Rise up, let us go." He walked with failures as if they had never failed.

Now since forgiveness means the restoration of a fellowship, it issues in newness of life. As forgiven we

13

thus walk with our Lord, we come more and more to share his divine nature. When, therefore, Jesus prayed for the forgiveness of his enemies, he was asking for them the best possible. He was asking for their regeneration. He was praying that they might experience his fellowship. He was praying that even these murderers might be able to shout with one of the greatest of the saints, "Old things are passed away; behold, all things are become new."

It is significant also that Jesus offered this prayer for the forgiveness of his enemies with complete confidence. He was perfectly sure that full forgiveness was available for every one of them. When he prayed for himself in the garden, he prayed with a condition, an "if" upon his lips, "If it be possible, let this cup pass from me." But here he did not ask the Father to forgive, if forgiveness was possible. He knew that forgiveness was already in his own heart. He knew that what he was offering, God was offering also. Thus Jesus in perfect confidence asked for heaven's best even for his enemies.

III

Then the Master gave a reason why the Father should grant his request: "Forgive them; for they know not what they do." On the surface it seems that Jesus was pleading a palliating circumstance. It was as if he were saying, "These men are doing a terrible wrong, but since they are sinning in ignorance, they are not so guilty as they seem." But this is not what Jesus meant. He was not

14

seeking to excuse their sin. The Bible is never eloquent in making excuses for sin. The individual who does so never wins his way into the presence of God. If you have an excuse for your sin, then you have a right to plead, "Not guilty." But if you dare make such plea, you will never be one inch closer to God than you are now. What, then, did Jesus mean by saying, "They know not what they do"?

He was not affirming that these who were doing him to death did not know that they were doing wrong. Such was not the case. They did know it, every man of them. Pilate, washing his soiled hands, did so in the realization that he had soiled his soul with the stain of a cowardly injustice. Judas, who hurried to empty his soiled hands of the thirty pieces of silver, in order to fill them with a hangman's rope, did so in the consciousness of his guilt. Annas, who had spun his web in the dark, knew that out of greed and envy he had helped to hound a good man to his death. There was not a man of them who with a clean conscience could plead, "Not guilty."

In what sense, then, were they ignorant? They were ignorant in that though they knew that they were doing wrong, they did not and could not realize just how great was their guilt. When Jesus said, "Father, forgive them; for they know not what they do," it was as if he had said, "Forgive them, for they need forgiveness so desperately. Forgive them, for they have committed a sin that is black beyond all their realization." That is doubtless true of

15

every sin we commit. We can never know what harvest we and others may have to reap because of one wrong decision or of one deed of disloyalty.

Thank God, this is also true on its brighter side. We can never know the high use that God can make of one right decision, of one word spoken in loyalty. A young physician called to see me a few years ago. "I became a physician," he declared, "because I knew that as such I would have the privilege of serving others, and as a Christian I was eager to do that." Then he asked, "Do you remember a walk we took together when I was in high school?"

"No," I answered with reluctance.

"Well, I remember it," he replied eagerly. "During that walk you spoke to me about becoming a Christian. As soon as we returned, I went to my room and surrendered to Christ."

What wonderful returns for so small an investment! We can never know, I repeat, the possible triumphant outcome of one right deed. No more can we know the possible tragedy of one wrong deed. Hence this prayer, "Forgive them," for their need was great beyond their knowing.

IV

If this prayer that our Lord offered in perfect confidence for God's best is to be answered for you and me, how are we to make that answer possible?

We must be willing to receive that forgiveness. That

we may be willing, we must realize our need. We must come confessing our sin. This is not a rigid rule passed by a narrow-minded God. It is the case in the nature of things. Only those who feel their need of forgiveness will give God a chance. Forgiveness is freely and eagerly offered to every man, but only those who know they have sinned and come short will be willing to accept this offer. Hence our gospel is a gospel for sinners, and for sinners only.

Our Lord enforced this truth by his most fascinating story. A father once prepared a feast to which both his sons were invited. One of these sons was a bit of a renegade, but the other was as decent as decency. While the younger had been a waster, the older had been a worker. When the younger son came home, his garments were stained with the filth of the swine pen. But the older son came with no stain upon him save the innocent soil of the fields. Naturally, this decent chap felt himself unmeasured leagues ahead of his prodigal brother. Not only so, but he had a right so to feel. Yet it was the prodigal who entered the banquet hall while his clean-living, hard-working brother shut the door in his own face.

Why was this the case? It was not because this father cared nothing for decency while he set a premium on profligacy. The door to the feast opened of its own accord to the prodigal because he came with this confession in heart and upon his lips, "I have sinned." That same door was shut in the face of his brother, shut by that

17

brother's own hand, because he came with this confession, "Lo, these many years do I serve thee, neither transgressed I at anytime thy commandment."

There you have it, two confessions: one, "I have *never* sinned"; the other, "I *have* sinned." Which is true? Which is yours? If the former, then you make this prayer of Jesus—this prayer that he offered both by his lips and by his cross—a sheer futility, so far as you are concerned. But if you come with this confession of sin upon your lips, if you come pleading

> Suffice it if—my good and ill unreckoned,
> And both forgiven thro' Thine abounding grace—

then a place at the feast of the fullness of life will be guaranteed to you.

The Second Word

"Verily I say unto thee, To day shalt thou be with me in paradise."

LUKE 23:43

THE FIRST WORD THAT JESUS UTTERED FROM HIS CROSS was a prayer for his enemies. This second word was an answer to prayer. It was an answer addressed to a single individual. Our Lord spoke to this man as if he were the only being in the world. What a satisfying answer he gave! What a strong staff he put into the hand of this dying man! What comfort this word must have brought! What comfort it has brought to countless needy souls since that far-off day! Of the seven words that Jesus spoke from his cross none, ~~I think~~, is more appealing and satisfying to my own heart than this: "To day shalt thou be with me in paradise."

I

Who offered the prayer that brought this satisfying answer?

The man to whom Jesus spoke this word is one of the most striking personalities that we meet upon the pages

19

of the New Testament. He was not a thief, in our sense of the word, but a revolutionist. He with his companion had belonged to the Jewish underground. Since they had not been able to organize armies and fight in the open, they had resorted to outlawry. They had organized guerrilla bands and had sought to prey upon Rome as ruthlessly as they felt that Rome had preyed upon them. Thus the man who offered the prayer that brought so rich an answer was a man of violence whose hands were deeply stained with human blood.

Nor was it by accident that our Lord was nailed to the central cross. That was a final malicious chuckle against Jesus on the part of his enemies. We can easily see the working of their minds. With a kind of fiendish glee they reminded themselves of the fact that throughout his ministry, Jesus had been a friend of sinners. They remembered how he had explained his having fellowship with Matthew and his brother renegades, by affirming that he had not come to call righteous people, but sinners. "All right," they sneered, "since he has made sinners his boon companions in life, we will give him the privilege of dying with them." Therefore they nailed him to the central cross.

One writer has suggested that this revolutionist had known Jesus before they met on the day of execution. One reason for believing this is that this outlaw addressed our Lord simply as Jesus. That is, he called him by the name that Mary called him when he was a boy in Nazareth. No other, so far as the record goes, ever

20

addressed our Lord in that fashion. They called him Master; they called him Jesus Master, Jesus of Nazareth, Jesus, thou Son of David. But none other ever called him simply by the name of Jesus.

I am inclined to agree, yet I realize that this revolutionist might have addressed our Lord in this fashion, not because he knew so much about him, but because he knew so little. If we assume that these two had never met before, then about all that this outlaw knew of the man on the central cross was what he had learned from the crowd, from hearing Jesus' prayer for his enemies, and from seeing his name on the cross above his head. While no two of the evangelists agree on the exact wording of the charge against Jesus, Matthew's version seems reasonable: "This is Jesus the King of the Jews." Had this man never met the Master before, he might not have prayed to him at all. But if with such little knowledge he had trusted him enough to pray to him, he would have called him Jesus, for that would have been all that he knew.

But whether or not Jesus and this outlaw had met before, they had much in common. They were both ardent patriots. They were both men of courage and of action. In a sense they had struggled toward a common goal. Both had sought to help their people. Jesus had done so to the end. The outlaw had doubtless done so till his career of violence had caused him to degenerate. They were also akin in that they had been willing to give them-

21

selves for the cause that they held dear. In many respects, therefore, they saw eye to eye.

But if they had much in common, they were also vastly far apart. In seeking to save his nation Jesus had refused to resort to violence. He had no faith in physical force. He had said to those who listened to him, "Resist not evil." He had declared that the man who took the sword would perish by the sword. He had even reached such a climax of absurdity that he said, "Blessed are the meek: for they shall inherit the earth." Naturally, to this revolutionist such teaching seemed sentimental nonsense. Rome had inherited the earth, and Rome was not meek. The only way out was to meet force with force, violence with violence. Thus with much in common, Jesus and this revolutionist were yet very far apart.

As to which of the two was right, we are by no means agreed to this day. The vast majority, however, still side with the man of violence. Yet the verdict of history is on the side of Jesus. He was sure that violence does not have the final answer. "He beheld the city, and wept over it." The sound of his sobbing comes to us from across the centuries. Why is he weeping? Because his people are too blind to see the things that make for peace. They are bent on winning by force, and Jesus knew that that would end in disaster. "For the days shall come upon thee, that thine enemies shall cast a trench about thee . . . and shall lay thee even with the ground, and thy children within thee; and they shall not leave in thee one stone upon another." That prophecy was literally fulfilled in less than fifty years. We are still by no means convinced that the meek will inherit the earth. But surely we have had to lose faith in the victory of the nonmeek. We have been forced to fear that if we do not cease to be violent, there will be no earth to inherit.

II

Why did this revolutionist pray?

He did not pray because he was frightened. He did not pray because he was seeking an easy way out of a hard situation. It was after this fashion that the lesser outlaw prayed. "If thou be Christ, save thyself and us." He did not suffer over being what he was; he suffered only in being where he was. But there is nothing of this mere seeking to escape in the prayer of this greater outlaw. Having taken the part of Jesus before he took his own, he asked not to be let off from suffering, but only to be remembered. His hell was in being what he was rather than in being where he was.

A recent writer for whom I have great respect affirms that we are wrong in calling this praying revolutionist penitent. He declares that the reason he prayed was he had had a vision of reality. Certainly he had had a vision of reality. But what had that vision done for him? What did a vision of reality do for youthful Isaiah? When he saw "the Lord . . . high and lifted up," he also saw himself. Having seen himself in the light of God, he did not like what he saw. Therefore he became penitent and cried: "Woe is me! . . . I am a man of unclean lips."

Against the white background of the innocence of Jesus this outlaw saw himself. Therefore he declared that though he was suffering the pangs of death, it was no more than he deserved. He was receiving the due reward of his deeds. A man who realizes that he deserves death knows that he has done something wrong. Had this man compared himself with the other revolutionist who was dying by his side, or had he compared himself with those howling churchmen who stood about the cross, he might have thought quite well of himself. But he could not feel that way once he had really seen Jesus.

Therefore I feel quite sure that his prayer was the prayer of a penitent. Whenever there is a sense of God, there is always a sense of sin. Not only so, but the more vivid the vision of God, the more poignant the sense of sin. To be convinced of this we need only to face the fact that the most tragic confessions of sin come, not from the lips of the greatest of sinners, but from those of the choicest of the saints. Throughout the centuries those men who have come closest to God are the ones who have poured forth confessions of sin that were most red with shame and wet with tears.

III

Look at the prayer of this repentant revolutionist. His prayer was addressed to Jesus, in whom he saw, not simply a king, but the King. What marvelous insight he had! This kingship of Jesus was the central sarcasm of that black hour. It was by accusing him of being a pretender that Annas and his crowd had brought about his condemnation. Pilate knew that the charge was false. He was therefore eager to set Jesus free. At times it looked as if he were going to succeed. But finally one shouted: "If thou let this man go, thou art not Caesar's friend." At that Pilate went hot and cold. He had to stand well with Caesar, cost what it might. Therefore he was afraid to release a man accused of being a pretender, even though he knew the accusation false.

When the underlings had seen that Jesus was condemned as a pretender, they took up the charge. The soldiers in their glee told themselves that a king must be properly dressed, so they put a scarlet robe on him. A king must have a scepter, so they put a reed in his hand. A king must have a crown, so they made him a crown of thorns. As a climax to the joke Pilate had placed this above his head, "This is Jesus the King of the Jews."

But to one man this kingship was no joke. With matchless insight this outlaw saw in the man who was dying at his side a King who could grant favors beyond death. Therefore he prayed, "Jesus, remember me when thou comest in thy kingdom."

This prayer was personal. The dying man was praying for himself. I know it is possible for us to be self-centered in our prayers. I know there are those who warn against praying for oneself. Yet to be so unselfish as to refuse ever to pray for yourself is to surpass your Lord. Jesus prayed for himself again and again. Of course we must pray for others. But we often fail to have either the inclination or the faith to pray for others till we have prayed for ourselves. The man who has cried, "God be merciful to me a sinner," and has received an answer is then the more ready to pray for his needy fellows.

This was a prayer of faith. In fact I think a more daring faith is hardly to be found in the Bible or out of it. He did not pray, "Remember me *if* thou comest in thy kingdom," but, "Remember me *when* thou comest." Then his faith was further indicated by the seeming modesty of his request. In fact his humility as contrasted with that of James and John, who asked for first places, was my first thought on reading his story. But he was making no modest request. So grandly did he think of Jesus that he was convinced that to have a place in his heart, to be remembered by him, was the very best that could be his, either in time or in eternity. Thus he asked for no throne, no seat among the mighty, only to be remembered.

IV

This prayer received an answer. It was an answer of assurance.

"Verily I say unto thee." No honest man could have spoken such a word unless he had been certain of the truth of what he was saying. Our Lord gave to this dying outlaw certain assurances that are as precious to us as they were to the man to whom he first gave them in the long ago.

1. Jesus here gave assurance that life goes on. He said

to this outlaw, "To day shalt thou be with me in paradise. As death cannot stop me, no more can it stop you." "To day shalt thou be." That means the survival of personality. George Eliot's dream of being immortal through the immortality of the human race is utterly futile. Our race is not immortal. Even though it might continue for a billion years, it is still headed toward utter extinction. But we live individually. Jesus knew that this revolutionist would still be himself beyond death. Even so, I will always be I; you will always be you.

2. Jesus here gave assurance of an abiding fellowship with himself. "To day shalt thou be with me." How had these two come to be together in the here and now? This repentant revolutionist was not with Jesus simply because he was on a cross so near him that had their hands been free, they could almost have touched each other. The lesser outlaw was just as close as the one to whom Jesus was speaking. These two had come together when this greathearted outlaw had prayed and received forgiveness. For to be forgiven as we saw in the first sermon is more than the removal of a penalty. It is the restoration of a fellowship. Together then, they would go on being together through time and through eternity.

3. Jesus here gave assurance of the heavenly home. He called the place of meeting paradise. In his conversation with his friends a few hours before, he had called it the house of many mansions. The saints of yesterday were accused of being too otherworldly. That is, they thought too much about the life to come and too little

27

of the life that now is. Such a charge could not possibly be brought against us. I am afraid that instead we are too hitherworldly. We need to brace ourselves with the certainty of the homeland of the soul. Personally I rejoice in the assurance that when Jesus stepped into God's house he had a redeemed revolutionist by the hand.

4. Jesus here gave assurance of the immediacy of our heavenly home. The belief that at death we fall asleep to wake at some far-off resurrection was not the faith of Jesus. It is not the faith of the New Testament. This is the shout of its saints, "Blessed are the dead which die in the Lord." Such are blessed at once because to be "absent from the body" is to be "present with the Lord."

5. Finally Jesus here gave assurance that those who turn to him are saved instantly. We do not have to wait for his pardon. It may be ours at once, even now.

A few years ago I was talking to a rather cultivated woman who seemed to know little of what it means to be a Christian. "Did you know," I asked, "that God has set a definite date for your salvation?" She looked a bit surprised and answered in the negative. "Well," I replied, "he has. If I show you that he has, will you keep your engagement with him?" After a moment she answered seriously that she would. "All right," I said, "here it is. 'Now is the accepted time; behold, now is the day of salvation.' "

If you will turn to him, you will be with him today. Being with him in the here and now, you can continue with him forevermore.

28

The Third Word

"Now there stood by the cross of Jesus his
mother. . . . When Jesus therefore saw his
mother, and the disciple standing by, whom
he loved, he saith unto his mother, Woman,
behold thy son! Then saith he to the disciple,
Behold thy mother!"

JOHN 19:25-27

THE FIRST WORD THAT JESUS SPOKE FROM THE CROSS
was a prayer for his enemies. The second, spoken to a
revolutionist who had become a friend, was an answer
to prayer. This third was addressed to Mary and to his
beloved disciple. Of all others, these were nearest to him
in loyalty and in devotion. Here we have his final message
to the two whom he loved best. To his mother he said,
"Behold thy son!" To the disciple, "Behold thy mother!"

I

While this word has in it something of the expected,
it has yet more of the unexpected.

In the light of the fact that Jesus shared the faith of
his people we are not surprised that he spoke here as a

29

family man, as a devoted and dutiful son. We can understand this when we bear in mind that Jesus was a member of a people that magnified family life to a superlative degree. The Jews believed that the family was a divine institution. They believed that "God setteth the solitary in families." They recognized the fact that children were not so much born as made. Therefore they gave particular emphasis to the high and solemn responsibility of parents. They affirmed that what a child becomes depends mainly upon his parents. "Train up a child in the way he should go: and when he is old, he will not depart from it." Jesus himself gave further emphasis to this responsibility by walling the child about by a wall of millstone, saying, "Whoso shall offend one of these little ones . . . , it were better for him that a millstone were hanged about his neck, and that he were drowned in the depth of the sea."

But if the Jews gave particular emphasis to the obligations of parents to children, they also emphasized the duty of children to parents. Ours is a day that has put the accent upon rights rather than upon responsibilities, but the two belong together. In the state, to claim the rights of a citizen one should be willing to discharge the obligations of a citizen. Even so in claiming the privileges of sonship one should be willing to discharge its obligations. This is true even of those who dare to remind their parents that they did not ask to be born and for that reason have no obligations. Of course they did not ask to be born, nor would their parents ever have asked for

30

them to have been if they had known they would become such moral nitwits. All rights involve obligations. This is true everywhere—in the state, in the church, in the home. Therefore the Jews strictly obeyed the command, "Honour thy father and thy mother."

That Jesus shared this faith is beyond doubt. This fact is indicated by his hot indignation against those religious leaders who permitted a son to refuse to support his parents if he would only declare that the substance that should have gone into this withheld support was given to God. But it was the conviction of Jesus that no service to others could atone for the neglect of one's parents. Paul was speaking to the same purpose when he said, "If any provide not for his own, and specially for those of his own house, he hath denied the faith, and is worse than an infidel." Therefore in providing for Mary, Jesus was simply doing the duty that was closest to him. Even the burden of a world's redemption could not obscure for him his loving obligation to his bereaved and widowed mother.

But if this devotion of Jesus to his mother is to be expected, what he actually said to her and to his best friend is, to me at least, somewhat surprising. This is the case because of both what he said and what he failed to say. Bear in mind that Jesus was dying. Bear in mind also that these were his last words on this side of death to the two whom he loved best. Under these circumstances I should have expected something more than a mere, "Behold thy son! . . . Behold thy mother!"

For instance, I should expect this devoted son to have given some hint to his perplexed mother of the meaning of his mysterious suffering. It seems that he might have reminded her that by thus dying he was to become the supreme magnet of the ages. What is perhaps stranger still, he said nothing to Mary of life beyond death. She was now getting well into years. She was not very long for this world. Yet he did not remind her of the house of many mansions of which he had spoken to his disciples. He did not say to her anything akin to the word that he had just spoken to the dying revolutionist. He made no mention of the certainty of a glad reunion beyond this world with its crosses, griefs, and graves.

Instead of comforting Mary by disclosing the after-life, Jesus spoke solely of the life that now is. He was concerned to provide for his mother, not simply in the beautiful by-and-by, but in the heartbreaking here and now. It is arresting to see how much of the earthly ministry of Jesus was devoted to providing for the physical needs of people. Even after he had risen from the dead, those hands that had throttled death were not above preparing breakfast for a few fishermen who had just come from a fruitless night of toil. Here on the cross he remembered that his mother must have bread and a place to live, not simply tomorrow, but today.

But in providing for Mary in the house of his beloved disciple, Jesus was doing more than merely seeing to it that she should have bread and shelter. He was providing her a home. Home is more than a place to live; it is a

32

place to love. Lacking this, home is just another name for hell. He knew that Mary would feel more at home in the house of this disciple than anywhere else; that this beloved friend would be able above all others to understand and to sympathize with her. Therefore he said, "Behold thy son! . . . Behold thy mother!"

Perhaps the most astonishing fact of all is that Jesus here told his mother to adopt another son when she already had four sons of her own. She also had at least two daughters. Since these sons and daughters had been trained by the same parents that had trained Jesus, they were no doubt loyal to the faith of their fathers. In all probability every one of them was a person of character and of standing in the community. Yet Jesus completely ignored them. He passed them by as if they were dead, and entrusted his mother to a friend.

II

Why did Jesus act in this strange fashion?

The fact that our Lord chose a friend to provide a home for his mother indicates a division in his own family. When Simeon took Jesus as a little child into his arms, he told Mary that a sword would one day pierce her heart because of that child. She found that saying tearfully true. Matthew tells us that Joseph, who is thought to have died when Jesus was in his early teens, was a just man. By this he does not mean that he was fair, but that he was an observer of the law. This zeal for the law was doubtless shared by Mary, and increasingly

33

by her children. So true was this in the case of James that he could become the leader of the church in later years without having to suffer persecution at the hands of his fellow Jews. But Jesus did not see eye to eye with his family in this matter of the law, as in various other particulars. Hence when he declared that a prophet has no honor in his own home, he was speaking out of a painful personal experience. Even Mary, in spite of her love for him and pride in him, could never quite understand him.

We see the first indication of this lack of understanding when Jesus as a lad went up to the Passover with Joseph and Mary. They lost him, and it was only after they had gone a day's journey that they missed him. Then they turned back in great anxiety to seek for him. When they found him in the temple, Mary asked with a tenderness that perhaps had in it a touch of impatience, if not of anger, "Why have you treated us like this?"

"Did you not know," came the reply of Jesus, "that I must be in my Father's house? You should have known where to find me since my first and supreme loyalty is not to you, but to God." Mary pondered all this in her heart, but she did not fully understand. Though she found her son and was privileged to have him with her after this for almost a score of years, yet there was a sense in which she failed to find him. Therefore she could never feel that he was altogether hers.

This lack of understanding seems to have persisted with the passing of the years. It shows up again at the wedding at Cana. Mary and Jesus were both present,

34

though as we read between the lines it would seem that they did not come together. When the wine gave out, Mary said to Jesus, "They have no wine." His answer seems downright shocking. According to Moffatt he said: "Woman, what have you to do with me?" This word is not as rude as it sounds. Yet Jesus was telling Mary as tenderly as he could that his orders came from above. "Henceforth," he seems to say, "the index finger that points to the hour at which I am to act will be that of no human hand, but of my Father."

I think that this chasm that divided Jesus from his own grew wider still when he preached his first sermon in his home church. The whole family were doubtless in the synagogue that morning, keenly eager for their kinsman to make a good impression. Both their family pride and their faith were involved. When, therefore, they heard "the gracious words" that Jesus spoke, their hearts fairly sang. But soon all this music was changed into discord. As if seeking to be offensive, the preacher told his congregation that in the long ago when God needed a boarding place for one of his greatest prophets he could not find one among the Jews, but had to go to a woman who lived in the land of Jezebel. He told them further that though God was able and eager to heal lepers, the only man in the days of Elisha who had faith to be healed was an outsider named Naaman. At this affront the congregation was changed into an angry mob and the preacher into a fugitive. How the faces of James and

35

Joseph, of Simon and Jude, must have burned! How the heart of Mary must have broken!

Of course after this his devout brothers were prepared to give ear to almost any wild rumor. Those rumors were plentiful enough. One that persisted and that they found quite credible was that Jesus was really crazy. Therefore there was nothing for them to do but to go and bring him home, and thus spare themselves further shame. They had no trouble in locating him. They came upon a great multitude and learned that he was at the center of it. Being unable to come at him because of the crowd, they sent word that they with their mother were waiting for him. But instead of coming and talking the situation over, he refused even to see them. That was the last straw. There was nothing they could do but go home without him. Mary went along with them because she was almost as much perplexed as they.

At last black shadows began to gather. Angry threats were blown on almost every breeze. It seemed that death might be drawing near. It was then that Mary could endure her position no longer. She left her other sons, who as John tells us did not believe in their brother, and hurried to stand by her first-born. She still did not understand him. Many things he did grieved and perplexed her. But in spite of all this she loved him with a love stronger than death. Therefore we read, "There stood by the cross of Jesus his mother." She took her stand by the cross, even though she had, in a sense, to break with her other children in order to be there.

Jesus therefore entrusted his mother to his friend because his own loved ones were *not* present. Then he entrusted his mother to this disciple because he *was* present. This beloved friend was standing by. He was near in person because he was near in love and loyalty. Being thus in the danger zone, in the zone of shame and suffering, he was also, for that very reason, in the zone of usefulness. Our Lord is shut up to using those who are nearest to him. He is shut up to using those who are near enough to be willing to hear and obey his voice. There was a sense in which Mary had to go to the home of this beloved disciple. There was simply nowhere else for her to go.

Yet it was an unspeakable honor for this friend to be so trusted and so used. He had the privilege of doing for Jesus what Jesus could not do for himself. He had the privilege of taking the place of his Lord in the service of one whom he loved. In one sense his privilege was unique. In a profounder sense it belongs to every one of us. There is never a day in which we cannot represent our Lord. There is never a day in which we cannot do something for him by doing something for one whom he loves. All that is necessary in order for us to enter into this high privilege is our own willingness.

III

Here, then, are the last words of Jesus to the two he loved the best: "Behold thy son! . . . Behold thy mother!" Then what?

Prompt obedience. These two loving hearts yielded to the will of Jesus without question. We read that from that hour this friend took Mary to his own home. "From that hour" might mean as soon as the crucifixion was over. It might also mean that he acted at once. I like to believe that this latter was the case. If I am right, it would mean that this beloved disciple lived not too far from Calvary. It would mean further that Mary in going at once from the cross was spared the agony of witnessing the final hour. It would be so like Jesus to desire to spare her this. Having thus found shelter in the home of her adopted son, she waited in the fellowship of those whose hearts broke with her own, till the black shadows of that Friday gave place to the radiance of Easter morning.

"Suppose ye that I am come to give peace on earth? I tell you, Nay; but rather division." The Master is here speaking out of his own experience. He created division among his own people and in his own family. But I love to remember that division is not his final word. He is the great uniter. He divided his family only to bring them together into a closer fellowship. When we see Mary after Easter on her way to Pentecost, she has with her not just one son, but five. Her adopted son is with her; so also are James and Joseph, Simon and Jude (Acts 1:14). These have come to accept Jesus, not only as a brother, but also as Saviour and Lord.

The Fourth Word

"My God, my God, why hast thou forsaken me?"

MATTHEW 27:46

THIS IS THE FOURTH WORD THAT JESUS UTTERED FROM his cross. It stands at the center of the seven. It seems to me altogether fitting that it should be so, for here the tragedy of the crucifixion reached its climax. We may be sure of the genuineness of these words. They carry their credentials in their own hands. No writer of fiction would have put such an utterance upon the lips of his hero. No one painting a face like that of Jesus would have marred his canvas by such a seeming blemish. "My God, my God, why hast thou forsaken me?" I wonder what impression these words made upon those who first heard them.

I

What impression did they make upon Annas and company? Here were hard men who through envy and political trickery had deliberately brought about the crucifixion of Jesus. Having accomplished their purpose,

39

they would not even suffer their victim to die in peace. They stood about the cross and jeered. They claimed that they would be willing to obey him if he would only vindicate his sonship to God by coming down from the cross. "He trusts in God," they flung at him. "Let God deliver him now, if he delights in him." But God did not deliver him. Not only so, but Jesus seemed to take their side by declaring himself forsaken.

I wonder what impression these words made upon the friends of Jesus. There were not many friends present, but there was at least one who had to be present. He was nailed to a cross beside that of Jesus. I am thinking of that new disciple who in the maddest possible adventure of faith had asked Jesus to remember him when he should come in his kingdom. Jesus had answered his prayer with the calm assurance of God himself: "To day shalt thou be with me in paradise." But where was that assurance now? He who a while ago had been so confident of his ability to win through and to take his friend with him must now have seemed little more than a blind man undertaking to lead the blind.

I remember a story that I read as a boy. I think it was in one of McGuffey's readers. It told of a gentleman who one day attended a country church where he heard a venerable minister preach an impressive sermon on the crucifixion. The minister contrasted the death of Jesus with that of Socrates. Over and over he rang the changes on this word: "Socrates died like a philosopher; Jesus Christ died like a God."

But is this wild outcry the outcry of a God? By no means. I am happy to say that the minister was wrong. Jesus Christ did not die like a God. He died like a man. That is the very center of our hope.

II

Why did Jesus utter this bitter cry?

I think the simplest explanation is the one that is true. He uttered it because he felt himself forsaken. There was nothing of the actor about Jesus. He was always perfectly sincere. He was not fighting a sham battle. If this was a sham battle, then it has no meaning for us because our battles are very real. Jesus was here speaking out of a sense of desolation. He felt that he was treading the wine press alone.

Not only so, but he felt that his forsakenness was utter and complete. He had been forsaken before this hour by the religious leaders among his own people. He had been forsaken by his family. At last he had been forsaken by his friends. But he had foreseen this last tragedy and had fortified himself against it by the assurance of the divine presence. "The hour . . . is now come, that ye shall be scattered, every man to his own, and shall leave me alone: and yet I am not alone, because the Father is with me." But now the Father's face was hidden. Thus he felt forsaken of God and man.

It was in this feeling of being forsaken that the horror of the cross reached its climax. Here was "the crucifixion within the crucifixion." Jesus found forsakenness hard

41

to bear because he was the most sensitive of men. He had a deep dread of loneliness. "Ye shall be scattered, every man to his own, and shall leave me alone: and yet I am not alone, because the Father is with me." No one would have said that except one who had a genuine horror of being left alone.

This loneliness was hard to bear, not only because Jesus was finely sensitive, but because it was in such sharp contrast to all that he had known before. It was so new in the experience of Jesus. A man who goes into the night from a brilliantly lighted room finds the darkness more depressing than if he went from a room lighted but dimly. Even so, no man misses the presence of God so much as one who has been keenly conscious of that presence through the years. Always God had been real to Jesus. Always he had been closer "than breathing, and nearer than hands and feet." But now that his Father's face was no longer seen, his heartache was by contrast all the sharper. After a day so full of brightness the darkness of this hour was all the blacker.

But that which brought this sense of forsakenness to its climax of bitterness was that it appeared to be without rhyme or reason. His suffering seemed for the moment so meaningless, so purposeless. We call this "The Cry of Dereliction." The word suggests a derelict ship. A derelict ship is one that has been abandoned. It has no captain. It has no crew. It has no compass. It has no cargo. It is bound for no port. Thus it has no meaning. Even so, for this black moment life seemed to Jesus little more than a meaningless suffering, with no high and holy purpose in it. That surely was "sorrow's crown of sorrow."

The experience of our tortured generation ought to help us to gain some understanding of this suffering of our Lord. We who are older remember the thrill of the First World War. How gallantly our soldiers went out to face conflict and death! This they did because they were sure of their goal. They were out to make the world safe for democracy. They were fighting a war to end war. They were going to usher in a new day. Therefore in spite of the suffering involved they went out singing. During the Second World War we were not so songful. And now as the clouds gather again many are bewildered and perplexed. It all seems so meaningless, even hopeless. Therefore I dare say that more bewildered souls are consciously or unconsciously asking this question today than ever before: "My God, my God, why?"

Good Lord - where are you

III

How did Jesus come by this conviction that he was forsaken?

Of course the full explanation is far beyond our powers. Here we can truly say to the very wisest, "Thou hast nothing to draw with, and the well is deep." But while we can only grope, we can do that. Of one fact, at least, we may be sure. It is this: our Lord was not in reality forsaken. On the contrary, God was never closer to his beloved Son than he was during this black hour.

43

That minister was right who, questioned by a bewildered father as to why God had let his son die a tragic death, answered that God was engaged in the same task when this man's son died that engaged him at the death of his own Son. He was in the midst of its black ugliness, sharing it and bringing out of it all possible good. The explanation of our fathers that God was here venting his wrath against sinners upon the sinless head of our Lord is an explanation that for us simply does not explain.

We find a further assurance that God had not forsaken Jesus in light of the fact he never forsakes anyone. Often we forsake him, but he never forsakes one of us, even the most hopeless rebel. When that foolish sheep had left the flock and had strayed into the wilds, the shepherd could not let it alone. He had to go seeking the silly creature until he found it. "God is like that," said Jesus. He never can stop until he finds us. Even when in our rebellion we enter the house of our own selfishness and slam the door in his face, he does not turn away. With unspeakable humility he still stands at the door and knocks. He never forsakes us however far we may go from him and however utterly we may rebel against him.

Therefore if God never forsakes one of his children, even the very worst, we may be sure that he did not forsake Jesus, whose one purpose in life had been to do the will of his Father. For God to have done so would have been utterly impossible. God has a character to support, even as you and I. When that psalmist of deep spiritual insight wrote, "He leadeth me in the paths of righteousness," he gave God's reason for so leading. That reason is not the one that I should have expected. He did not say, "He leadeth me because I am blind and ignorant." No more did he say, "He leadeth me because he knows that if I should go astray I might lead others astray." But here is the reason he gave: "He leadeth me in the paths of righteousness for his name's sake." God's character demands that he lead those who trust him in right paths till they come victoriously to a right goal.

Furthermore, for God to forsake one who trusted him would be to give the lie to every promise that the saints of the centuries have heard from his lips. The one characteristic of God which those who have ventured upon him are most sure of is his faithfulness. They declare with one voice that he will never let us down. They are convinced with a conviction born of experience that he can be depended upon to the uttermost. "I will never, never leave thee, nor forsake thee," is with them not a mere theory, but a tested fact. Cast down they often are, but forsaken never. This assurance of God's trustworthiness has sung its way through all the troubled centuries. Therefore we may be perfectly sure that the sinless Jesus was not forsaken upon the cross.

If we are right, how can we explain this sense of forsakenness? That Jesus felt forsaken is beyond question. I think it came about in part through his physical torture. Let us not forget that Jesus was a man. Let us not forget that he was just as human as we are. Many in our day have discovered afresh the terrible effect that torture may have upon the very strongest. Russia has demonstrated again and again through her cruel persecutions how even men of integrity and strength may be made to confess wrongs of which they know nothing. Torture weakens the whole man. Jesus had had to suffer terribly. He had endured four mock trials. He had been tried before Annas, Caiaphas, Herod, and Pilate. He had been crowned with thorns. He had been scourged. He had been now upon the cross for almost six hours. It is not surprising that this physical suffering had told in some measure upon his vivid sense of God. Any man who for long hours has felt pain walk with fire-shod feet along every nerve of his body knows how easy it is to lose a sense of the divine presence.

But the full reason why Jesus came to feel himself forsaken is, I repeat, beyond our human understanding. But of this much the writers of the New Testament are certain. Here on the cross Jesus was made "to be sin for us, who knew no sin." I think there is no doubt that our Lord recognized himself as the suffering servant of Jehovah. Here he was being wounded for our transgressions and bruised for our iniquities. "He saved others," his enemies shouted at him, "himself he cannot save." One hell from which he could not save himself and be our Saviour was this sense of forsakenness.

If this fact perplexes us, if it is beyond our understanding, it also gives us hope.

46

There was the Door to which I found no Key;
There was the Veil through which I might not see.

We too come to doors to which we find no key and veils
through which we cannot see. The facile comfort given
by those who have lived all their lives on the sunny side
of the street may help little. In fact it may be positively
irritating. But when we find one who has deeply suffered
and has come through with a vital faith and a tender
heart, to such we listen gladly. Here is one secret of the
spell that our Lord casts over men. "In that he himself
hath suffered being tempted, he is able to succour them
that are tempted."

IV

Now what did Jesus do when his black hour was upon
him?

He did not fall down in self-pity and give over the
fight. No more did he declare in stubborn bitterness that
he would see the hard ordeal through in his own strength.
Instead he did what had been the habit of his life. He
turned to God in prayer.

I know that this grim word is a question. It is, so far
as the record goes, the only question that Jesus ever addressed to God. But that fact did not prevent it from
being a prayer. It was a prayer offered in faith. It was
offered with the conviction that God was still his very
own. "My God," he prayed. As long as we can claim
God as our very own, we cannot be utterly desolate.

47

Not only did Jesus pray in the faith that God was still his very own, but he prayed in the faith that God knew the answer to his perplexing question and that in his love he would give him the answer. So what? The God in whom he trusted did not let him down. He did not disappoint him. Having thus prayed, Jesus received an answer that enabled him to see the remainder of this crucifixion journey through with a quiet heart and with a serene mind. Having thus prayed, he was able to reach the end, not with a wail of despair, but with a shout of victory.

Here, then, is a word for every one of us. It is especially dear to those who have found life bewilderingly hard. Our Lord helps us by every word that he uttered from his cross. We can thank God for every one of them. But I am sure that there are many fine and sensitive and tortured souls who thank God for this word above all else, "My God, my God, why hast thou forsaken me?"

The Fifth Word

"*After this, Jesus knowing that all things were now accomplished, that the scripture might be fulfilled, saith, I thirst.*"

JOHN 19:28

I THIRST. JESUS DID NOT UTTER THIS WORD, AS A SUPER-ficial reading of the text might suggest, in order to fulfill the scriptures. Had such been the case, our Lord would have been little better than an actor, and he never put on an act. The assertion "that the scripture might be fulfilled" is the affirmation of a result rather than of a purpose. If Jesus did not utter this word to fulfill the scriptures, still less did he utter it as an appeal for pity. Jesus hated being pitied, as strong souls ever do. It was because of this hatred that he rebuked those women who sobbed over him as he journeyed to his cross. No more was this a grim bulletin announcing how the sufferer was faring as he did his last mile. Least of all was it a half-crazed cry that agony surprised from his unwilling lips.

Jesus was fully conscious of saying this word, as he

49

was of saying every other word that he spoke upon his cross. Indeed we may be certain that the principal reason for his refusing the medicated wine that was offered him before his crucifixion was that he might meet his ordeal intellectually alert and alive. He was determined to keep his faculties unbeclouded to the very end. This he did. Therefore Jesus knew exactly what he was saying when he cried, "I thirst."

In my opinion he was here once more engaged in prayer. But this prayer he offered, not to his Father, but to men. What is stranger still, he offered it to men who, either in cruel indifference or in vindictive hate, were making his last moments as bitter as possible. If this is a prayer, what an amazing prayer this is! It is also as beautiful as it is amazing.

<h1 style="text-align:center">I</h1>

Let us look at the beauty of this prayer.

1. It is beautiful in that it breathes a spirit of forgiveness. Some of us do not like to ask favors of anybody. But if we do have to ask favors, we desire to ask them only of those who are our friends. We certainly do not like to ask favors of those who have wronged us or who are hostile to us. The other day a father said to his son, who had become very much offended: "If you ever need my help, I will be glad to give it."

That son answered bitterly, "I would rather die of starvation than ask help from you."

Jesus was not like that. He was so forgiving that he was willing to ask a favor from even an enemy.

2. This prayer is beautiful in its humility. The man who was thus asking his enemies for a drink of water had been taunted for hours by having the fact of his weakness, his inability to save himself, flung into his face. Had Jesus been as proud as he was courageous, he would have died rather than confess that his enemies were right in affirming his human frailties. But he was not proud. Therefore he virtually took the side of his foes by confessing his need and throwing himself upon their generosity.

This was not the first time that Jesus had asked a drink of water from one who was not friendly: "There cometh a woman of Samaria to draw water: Jesus saith unto her, Give me to drink." But she looked at him with hard eyes and questioned, "How is it that thou being a Jew asketh drink of me, which am a woman of Samaria? for the Jews have no dealings with the Samaritans." Jesus answered, "If thou knewest the gift of God, and who it is that saith to thee, Give me to drink; thou wouldest have asked of him, and he would have given thee living water."

This was too much for the woman to believe. Therefore she asked him in amazement, "Art thou greater than our father Jacob, which gave us the well, and drank thereof himself, and his children, and his cattle?" "Infinitely greater," Jesus seemed to reply. "Whosoever drinketh of this water shall thirst again: . . . but the water

51

that I shall give him shall be in him a well of water spring-
ing up into everlasting life."

Yet this man who claimed the ability to give an in-
ward and unfailing spring was not too proud to ask for
water at the soiled hands of an outcast woman or from
the bloody hands of his murderers.

3. This prayer is beautiful in its faith in man even at
his worst. In fact it reminds me of that trustful prayer
that Martha and Mary offered for Lazarus, their sick
brother. When they realized that this illness might prove
serious, they did the most natural thing possible; they
turned to Jesus, their wise and understanding friend. But
in so doing they did not give him a blueprint of what he
was to do. They simply told him, "He whom thou lovest
is sick." It was their way of saying, "We know that you
love our brother; we know that you love us. Therefore
we leave our case in your hands with the firm faith that
you will do what is wisest and best."

It was in somewhat similar fashion that Jesus prayed.
He did not make his appeal to some single friendly face
that he saw in the crowd. He did not point out the
sponge, the reed, and the wine, and tell his helper what
to do. He simply stated his need and left it there. It was
a prayer, I repeat, akin to that of Martha and Mary, yet
there was this wide difference: the two sisters were praying to one who was a friend, while Jesus was praying to
those most of whom were even then howling with glee
over his torture. He had a faith in God that nothing could

kill, not even the cross. What is stranger still, he also had a deathless faith in men.

Without this amazing faith Jesus could never have become the world's Redeemer. The author of the letter to the Hebrews tells us that Christ "for the joy that was set before him endured the cross." He rejoiced in that grim instrument of torture because he was sure that his suffering would not be in vain. Knowing the human heart as he knew it, he never doubted that, lifted up from the earth, he would draw all men unto himself.

As this faith in man sent Jesus courageously to his task, even so it assisted him in performing that task. Such a faith is as needful for us as it was for our Lord. If we conclude with the cynic that the crooked can never be made straight, that conviction will tend to kill all earnest effort to help. Not only so, but even if we seek to help, our efforts are not likely to prove victorious. Generally speaking, the measure of a man's power to help his brother is the measure of the love in the heart of him and of the faith that he has that at last the good will win. Often, therefore, the very finest service that we can render our friends and our loved ones—husband, wife, and child—is just to believe in them. Here, then, is a prayer that Jesus offered in a spirit of forgiveness in humility and with a fine faith in men.

II

When did Jesus offer this prayer?

We find the answer in this twenty-eighth verse: "After

this, Jesus knowing that all things were now accomplished, that the scripture might be fulfilled, saith, I thirst."

That is, Jesus offered this prayer when the worst of his hard ordeal was behind him. When he came close to the end of his crucifixion journey, he became mindful of his own needs. We have a similar word in the Gospel of Matthew: "When he had fasted forty days and forty nights, he was afterward an hungred." During the days of his conflict Jesus was so absorbed in his battle with the tempter that he was not conscious of his hunger. It was only when the battle was over that he felt its gnawing pain.

An athlete in the course of an exciting game may receive a painful wound and be for the moment unconscious of it. But when the game has been played to the finish, then that wound will announce its presence. Some time ago I witnessed an all but fatal automobile accident. The driver of the car received a cut on the head that made his face red with blood. His wife and small boy were both knocked unconscious. Yet this man remained as cool and self-possessed as if nothing had happened. He telephoned for an ambulance. When it came, he rode with his wife and boy to the hospital sixty miles away. There he continued to be utterly free from nervousness till his loved ones were in bed and under the care of a physician. Then, knowing that he had done all he could, he went home and to bed for some much needed rest. But instead of resting he found himself in the grip of such a rigor as he had never known before. Even so Jesus had been so absorbed in other matters that he had not had time to think upon his own pain and upon his own needs.

First he had been concerned for those immediately about him. He had been concerned for those enemies for whom he had prayed. He had been concerned for the outlaw who had made his appeal to be remembered. He had been concerned about his bereaved mother. Jesus was bearing the burdens not only of those immediately about him, but of the whole world. Thus thinking upon others he had no time to think of himself. Many of those who are suffering today would forget much of their agony if they were to become deeply interested in the needs of others. It is wonderful how an effort to dry the tears of a neighbor will cleanse our own cheeks of their painful rain.

This fact gives us some insight into the nature of the sufferings of Jesus. His pain was not so much physical as mental and spiritual. It also gives us some small appreciation of the intensity of that agony. Death by crucifixion was about the most painful mode of torture that the fiendish ingenuity of man could contrive. That which brought this anguish to its climax was the burning thirst that it engendered through bloodletting. Hunger may be painful, but it is as starlight to sunlight in comparison to the pangs of thirst. Yet so great was his anguish of spirit that it was not till he had realized that all things were now accomplished that he prayed for water. Even the hot hell of thirst could not claim the attention of our Lord till he had won through. But having gained the victory, he was then eager to receive whatever help human hands could give. Hence he cried, "I thirst."

III

What came of this prayer?

Had I been present, perhaps in my cynicism I should have expected nothing to come of it. Yet I have to face this fact: Across the years I have sometimes been surprised at the lack of kindness on the part of some from whom I felt I had a right to expect it. But far more often I have been surprised by the kindness of others from whom I felt I had the right to expect nothing at all. How many times have strangers whose faces I had never seen before warmed my heart and made me half shamed by their unexpected kindness!

On a train the other day I saw an embarrassed little mother who was having a terrible time with a big yearling of a boy. The two were attracting the attention of everybody in the coach. I think almost everybody was sympathetic with the harassed mother, but nobody dared do anything about it. Yes, there was one exception. A husky chap who looked as if he might just have come from a wheat threshing took a hand. He bought some fruit and approached the bawling brat and said, "Here, put this down your neck." It was not very delicate language, but the howling yearling understood. He took the fruit and proceeded to put it down his neck, and there was a great calm. But what warmed my heart most was not the resulting quietness, but the kindness of the chap who took the mother's burden upon himself.

After Jesus had uttered this prayer for water, things continued for the moment just about as they had been before. The rabble still howled; a few were interested and sympathetic, but they did nothing about it. They only said, "Wait, let's see. Maybe that chap Elijah will come and help." But there was one man who simply could take it. His kindness drove him into action. His action was immediate. He said, "This man is suffering intensely now. Not only so, but if I do not help him now, I can never help him because the end is very near." So we read of him that he ran.

Who was this soldier who served Jesus so beautifully in his last moments? Frankly we do not know his name. He was so busy doing his act of kindness that he failed to leave us his autograph. Yet I am sure that there is one place where his name is not forgotten. I am certain that it is recorded in the Lamb's Book of Life. Jesus was able to say to him a little later, with bold literalness, "I was thirsty and you gave me drink."

Now, if any of you have it in your hearts to envy this nameless soldier, I have for you this encouraging word. Such an opportunity is also yours even now. This is the case because Jesus is still on the cross. This episode on Calvary represents the eternal heartache of our Lord for the suffering of his people. He is still being crucified through the agony of those about us. If we have the

57

heart to minister to them, we shall in no case lose our reward. One day Jesus will say to us, "I was thirsty, and ye gave me drink. . . . Inasmuch as ye have done it unto one of the least of these my brethren, ye have done it unto me." Man, what a chance!

The Sixth Word

"It is finished."

JOHN 19:30

FINISHED. THIS WORD SPOKEN BY OUR LORD AS HE HUNG
on the nails might have been the saddest that ever fell
from human lips. He might thus have been putting a
bloody period to a life whose dearest dreams and holiest
hopes had ended in utter failure.

In the far north at the foot of Mount McKinley a
skeleton was found seated on the root of a tree. Just above
was a finger carved in the bark, pointing down to the
skeleton. Beside the finger were these words: "The end
of the trail." They told the tragic story of one who had
set out to climb that lofty mountain, but his strength had
failed. He had died with his purpose unrealized.

Even so, by this word "finished" Jesus might have
meant simply that he himself had reached the end of his
trail. He might have thus been saying, "I am through. I
have gone my limit, having won nothing but shame and
defeat and death." But this word is not in reality a wail of
despair. On the contrary it is a shout of triumph. It was
uttered in the thrill of an irrepressible joy.

59

I

What is the secret of the joy that caused Jesus to speak this word?

He was not here rejoicing, as some have hinted, merely because he had reached the end of his earthly journey. Jesus was a normal man. He was a healthy man. As such he enjoyed the life that now is. As such he had a normal man's clinging to life. He was not so constantly homesick for his Father's house that he found no gladness in this present world. Those who call the here and now a "vale of tears," those who make

> Earth is a desert drear,
> Heav'n is my home,

their theme song, certainly do not agree with Jesus. As God called this world good on the day of creation, so Jesus thought of life as good.

That our Lord found this present life joyous is evident to any candid reader of the New Testament. He had certain gladsome words upon his lips again and again. One of them was this: "Be of good cheer." How futile it would have been for Jesus to have spoken in this fashion to troubled and perplexed men had his own face been black with despair. Another word was "blessed." "Oh, the blessedness, the gladness of the merciful," he shouted. "Oh, the joy of the meek, the happiness of the pure in heart." Jesus lived these beatitudes before they became articulate upon his lips. He knew through his own experience the joy that they express. I am not forgetting that he was "a man of sorrows, and acquainted with grief." But that fact did not prevent his being anointed with the oil of gladness above his fellows. It is my conviction that his was the sunniest face that ever looked out on this world and his the gladdest heart that ever beat in a human's bosom.

We can believe this, not only because of the New Testament record, but because it makes excellent sense. Jesus lived a consecrated life. He lived a life completely dedicated to the will of God. If I were to become convinced that the more completely one gave himself to God, the more miserable one would become, it would be very difficult for me to believe in God at all. Since Jesus lived a perfectly dedicated life, it was only natural that he should be the most joyous of men. He was joyous, not only during the springtime of his ministry when it looked as if victory was going to be easy; he was joyous to the very end. When the clouds gathered and he bowed with his disciples for their last prayer together, that prayer had in it this petition: "That they might have my joy fulfilled in themselves."

Since Jesus found life so joyous, it is very natural that he was not eager to leave it. He shrank from the ordeal of death, even as you and I.

> For who, to dumb forgetfulness a prey,
> This pleasing anxious being e'er resign'd,

Left the warm precincts of the cheerful day,
Nor cast one longing, ling'ring look behind?

Jesus therefore was not rejoicing simply because he had reached the end of his earthly journey. He loved life, and lived it with a glad and gallant heart.

The joy of Jesus was the joy of a man who had completed a task of supreme worth. He had not merely brought this task to an end; he had finished it. His victory was not partial, as is always the case with ours. The picture that he had painted was one to which he would not have added a single stroke. It was a picture from which he would have erased nothing. Just as Jesus a few hours before had said to the Father, "I have finished the work which thou gavest me to do," even so he was now shouting that same triumphant word from his cross. He was rejoicing over the finishing of the greatest of all tasks.

II

What was this task that Jesus had finished? What had our Lord come to do? To this question the Gospels give more than one answer. Look at a few of them.

1. "The Son of man is come to seek and to save that which was lost." He claimed that as a good physician he had come to attend, not those who were well, but those who were ill. He had come to save all the lost of the whole world. He had come to fulfill the sermon of the

angelic minister: "For unto you is born this day . . . , a Saviour, which is Christ the Lord."

2. "I am come that they might have life, and that they might have it more abundantly." As we turn the pages of the New Testament, we cannot help seeing that Jesus fairly cast a spell over the men of his day. One secret of that spell was that they found him so vital. He was beautifully alive. Again and again they came to him to ask him about life. One day a young aristocrat dared in the face of the crowd to kneel at his feet to put his question: "What shall I do that I may inherit eternal life?" "I want a quality of life," he seems to say, "that will be good today and good tomorrow and good to the end of time and good to the end of eternity. How can I find it?" Jesus knew the answer and gave it. He came that we might have life.

3. Jesus came in quest of a kingdom. He came to build men into a brotherhood. He came that we might say of men and nations what Luke said of the saints after Pentecost: "The multitude of them that believed were of one heart and of one soul." He declared that this brotherliness was the hallmark of vital Christianity. "By this shall all men know that ye are my disciples, if ye have love one to another." He came to build a kingdom of right relations. He came to bring about that high consummation, the doing of the will of God on earth, even as it is done in heaven.

4. The all-inclusive reason for which Jesus came was to reveal God. "No man hath seen God at any time; the

63

only begotten Son, which is in the bosom of the Father, he hath declared him." It was to make God known that Jesus came. Therefore if we desire to know what God is like, we can find our answer in Jesus. Nor could we possibly imagine a more satisfying answer. When Paul sought to say the best that he could say about God, he said that he was the Father of our Lord Jesus Christ. That is, God is like Jesus. Jesus revealed God by what he did upon the cross. Here on Calvary we see God's supreme revelation of himself.

III

Certain of our fathers used to call this "the finished work of Christ." In what sense were they correct?

Our Lord's work was not finished in the sense that in suffering love he is no longer seeking to save that which is lost. This tragedy on Calvary is a historic event that took place at a certain date on the calendar. But it is far more. It is a revelation of the eternal heartache of God for his children. It is a picture of what our Lord has suffered and does suffer and will continue to suffer till he finds and brings to his fold the sheep that have gone astray. But Christ's work is finished in that here on this skull-shaped hill he has given a revelation of suffering love that is final and ultimate. Beyond this not even the Son of God can go.

It is also easy to treat this finished work in a trite and wooden fashion as it applies to us. "Jesus Paid It All" holds in its hands a great and comforting truth. It may

64

voice the glad faith of those who, having freely received, are eager freely to give. But it may also be the song of those who are too grasping to give either of their substance or of themselves. This word, "the finished work of Christ," is not out of harmony with Paul's admonition, "Work out your own salvation with fear and trembling." No more does it contradict that strong boast, "I . . . fill up that which is behind of the afflictions of Christ in my flesh."

What did Paul mean by this latter word? He did not mean that this suffering of our Lord on Calvary was incomplete or inadequate. He was simply affirming that a sacrificial Saviour must have a sacrificial minister to proclaim him adequately. He was saying that a Christ who has given himself to the uttermost must have a disciple who will give himself to the uttermost if that disciple is to achieve his highest usefulness. He is asserting with a fellow apostle, "He laid down his life for us: and we ought to lay down our lives for the brethren."

> Love so amazing, so divine,
> Demands my soul, my life, my all.

IV

"Finished." Since God through Christ has made, and is making, perfect provision for the salvation of all men, what are we to do?

We must face the fact that the realization of that salvation waits upon our co-operation. My father was a farmer. He was a Christian farmer. But the fact that he was a Christian did not mean that when the springtime came he prayed God to turn the soil and to sow wheat in one field and to plant corn in another. He prayed me to do that. He was wise enough to know that in spite of God's provision, both he and his family would starve if he refused to do his part.

It is certainly the will of God that we should have a peaceful and brotherly world. God has made provision for such a world, but he cannot realize his holy purpose without our co-operation. He is eager for a church that shall indeed be a glorious church without spot or blemish, but he cannot have such a church without our help. He longs with the very passion of Calvary that you and I shall be Christlike, that the beauty of the Lord shall rest upon us as the sunshine rests upon the hills. He has made provision for such Christlikeness, but that provision will go for nothing if we fail to do our part.

What, then, I repeat, are we to do? We are to bear in mind that our Lord is saying to us what he said to his friends in the long ago, "This is my body; this is myself, given for you and to you." Since this is true, we are to receive him as a gift. We are to do this in the realization that by so doing we receive power to become sons of God. Having thus received power to become, we also receive power to serve.

Hudson Taylor tells us that one holiday when he was a youth in his teens he was left alone. Time hung rather heavily on his hands. Therefore he hunted for something to read. He found a tract in which he was interested only because he knew there would be a story in it. But as he read this tract, he came for the first time upon this word, "the finished work of Christ." It laid hold of his youthful heart. "Then there dawned upon me the conviction," he writes, "that there was nothing for me to do but fall upon my knees, accept the Savior, and praise him for evermore."

In so saying, Hudson Taylor spoke a great truth. But of course he was the furthest possible from affirming that having accepted Christ there was nothing else for him to do. The amazing work that he accomplished is sufficient answer to that. He was only declaring with the saints of the centuries that salvation is not something to be earned, but a gift to be received. "The wages of sin is death; but the gift of God is eternal life." This eternal life is nothing less than God through Christ giving himself. Our Lord does not save us and then give himself. He saves by the giving of himself. We can be saved in no other way. We might be able to find reformation in our own strength, but we can be transformed only by receiving Jesus Christ and permitting him to transform us from within.

Here, then, in this finished work of Christ is the answer to our supreme needs and to our deepest longings. For to receive him is to find satisfaction for the thirsts of the soul. Not only so, but it is also to find satisfaction for our longing to serve. Everybody wants to count. "The sense of uselessness is the greatest shock that can come to a living organism." But by receiving Christ we find our highest usefulness. "He that believeth on me . . . out of his [inner life] shall flow rivers of living water." Therefore since our Lord is inviting us to come to him and to receive his best, we ought to answer with joyful confidence,

> Just as I am, without one plea,
> But that thy blood was shed for me,
> And that thou bidd'st me come to thee,
> O Lamb of God, I come, I come!

The Seventh Word

"Father, into thy hands I commend my spirit."

LUKE 23:46

I

FATHER, INTO THY HANDS I COMMEND MY SPIRIT. THIS IS the final word that our Lord uttered from his cross. Not only does this word tell us how Jesus died, but it also tells us how he lived. Charles Lamb wrote of a friend: "Who parted this life on Wednesday evening; dying as he had lived, without much trouble." What Lamb said of his friend is true of mankind in general. As a rule men die as they live. There is nothing in the mere act of passing that makes a bad man good, or a good man bad. Generally we die as we live. So it was with Jesus.

I was reading some years ago of a man who made himself famous in the restaurant business. He established restaurants all the way across our continent. When at last he reached the end of his earthly journey, those nearest to him gathered about his bed to hear his final words. When they bent over him to catch his last whisper, it was this: "Slice the ham thin." There was nothing necessarily wicked about such a final word. It means only that his ruling passion was strong in death.

Not so long ago I was called to see a man who was desperately ill. Though he had largely wasted his substance in riotous living, when he realized that he was coming close to the end, he called for a minister. I went and, in the language of John Wesley, "offered him Christ." Not only so, but I believe that despite the lateness of the hour that offer was accepted. He seemed to receive it with joy, and his loved ones who stood about the bed rejoiced with him. But when a little later he became unconscious and then slipped away, his last word was not a prayer, but an oath. Of course he did not know what he was saying. But so long had he schooled his tongue in the language of blasphemy that he swore spontaneously. Generally speaking, I repeat, we die as we live.

As this is true on the dark side, so it is on the bright. I heard Dr. Edwin McNeill Poteat tell this bit about the home-going of his saintly father, who was also an able minister of the gospel. When this good man realized that he was close to the sunset, he called Edwin McNeill to his bedside and told him of his coming exodus. Then he requested of his son that he conduct his funeral services. "I realize," he continued, "that I am giving you a rather difficult assignment. But," he added, "if you will conduct my services this time, I promise never to ask you to do it again." I like that. So long had this saintly man lived in the fellowship of his Lord that he could even face

70

death with a twinkle in his eye. Thus he died as he lived, in joyful confidence.

II

"Father, into thy hands I commend my spirit." As this word sums up the death of Jesus, so, I repeat, it sums up his life. As his robe was woven of one piece, so also his life was of one piece. There was no break between his living and his home-going. To be convinced of this we need only to turn afresh to the pages of the New Testament. Here we see that what Jesus did in his final moments he had been doing throughout the years.

1. In this word, "Father, into thy hands I commend my spirit," Jesus is quoting from the thirty-first psalm. In his final hour he turned to the hymnbook of his people. But this turning to the scriptures was nothing new in the life of our Lord. This was not the first time since he had come to the cross that he made use of this book. His cry of dereliction, though so fully his own that we tend to forget that it was first uttered by lesser lips, is also a quotation from the Psalms. In fact our Lord had so saturated his mind and heart with the Bible that both its thought and its language became his own.

For instance, when people came to him with questions, he would often ask, "Have ye not read?" or, "How readest thou?" When a certain lawyer asked him to tell what was the supreme commandment, Jesus did not express an opinion of his own; he simply referred his questioner to the Old Testament. On another occasion the Sadducees, who did not believe in the resurrection, and who accepted only the first five books of the Bible, came to him with this rather comical story: There were seven brothers who, from the oldest to the youngest, had consecutively married a certain woman. Now, since they all married her, this was the question: If there is a resurrection, whose wife is she going to be? Personally, I have never felt that there would be any great contest for her. But that is not the point. The point is that Jesus answered that part of their story that had to do with the resurrection with a quotation from the book of Exodus.

As Jesus used the Bible for the instruction of others, even so he made use of it in the living of his own life. When I visited Mount Vernon, I was interested in the sword with which Washington armed himself during the Revolutionary War. The Old Testament was the sword of the Spirit with which Jesus fought his battles. Every onslaught of the enemy during his struggle in the wilderness he repelled by a thrust of this keen blade. It was only natural, therefore, that Jesus in his last hour should turn afresh to the book that had been his constant companion through his entire life. There was about it a beautiful spontaneity.

2. This word is a prayer. Jesus did not use the exact words of the scriptures. He added one word of his own. That was "Father." As our Lord had made a habit of saturating his mind with the Bible, so he had made a habit of prayer. He had taught men to pray by what he said. He had taught them also by what he did. In fact if we

72

take the Gospels as our guide, we discover that the only work that ever really taxed the energies of Jesus was the work of prayer. After he prayed, everything else seemed to come as a matter of course. From the place of prayer he went as a victor to receive the spoils of his conquest. Having thus practiced prayer day by day, Jesus found it perfectly natural to pray as he reached the end of his journey.

3. This prayer was an act of dedication. It was a committal. Moffatt gives this translation: "I trust my spirit to thy hands." This committal of himself to God was also a habit of Jesus. His Bible reading and prayer helped to this end. "I consecrate myself," is a part of the last prayer that he prayed with his disciples. Always he could say, "The Father hath not left me alone because I do always the things that please him." After he had made the commitment of himself to his Father a fixed habit of his life, it was only natural for him to fall asleep with this prayer upon his lips, "Father, into thy hands I commend my spirit."

III

"Father, into thy hands I commend my spirit." As these words sum up what both life and death meant to Jesus, they also sum up what they ought to mean to us. If we make this committal to God the habit of our lives, then we may be sure that such habit will stand us in good stead, both when we are in the thick of the fight and when we come to the end of our earthly journey. "I trust my spirit to thy hands." This is the whole meaning of our Christian religion. This is the least we can do and be Christian at all. It is the most we can do, either in time or in eternity.

1. Committal is the doorway into the kingdom. How do we become Christians? Our experiences are varied since God is a God of variety. We do not all react in the same fashion. But there are characteristics of conversion that are common to all of us. They are obedience, surrender, dedication. We enter by the door of commitment because there is none other.

Take Paul, for instance. When we read these thrilling words: "I saw in the way a light from heaven, above the brightness of the sun, shining round about me and them which journeyed with me," we say, "Of course Paul was converted after an experience like that. If I were to see such splendor in my sky, I too would be converted." But this would not necessarily be the case.

Paul might have gone from the brightness of the light of this vision into a deeper darkness than he had ever known before. This vision no more saved Paul than the sight of a laughing spring would save a man who was dying of thirst. Before the thirsty man can be saved, he must kiss the spring on the lips. Before Paul could be saved, he had to obey. He sums up his secret in one single sentence: "I was not disobedient unto the heavenly vision." The great apostle therefore entered the kingdom through the door of committal.

There was another apostle whose conversion was just

74

as real as that of Paul. Yet how commonplace his story seems! "As Jesus passed . . . , he saw a man, named Matthew, sitting at the receipt of custom: and he saith unto him, Follow me." Then what? We read the answer in this simple sentence: "And he arose, and followed him." Did he pray? Did he laugh? Did he sob? Did he shout and sing? We are not told. We are told only that he obeyed. He made a committal of himself. Thus he entered the kingdom.

That is the door that we must enter, for there is none other. Here was a lovely young aristocrat who was a far finer man than Matthew. He had almost everything in his favor. He was clean, courageous, and religious. Yet when Jesus gave him the same invitation that he gave to Matthew, when he said, "Follow me," the young ruler did not make the same response. Instead we read of him this tragic word, "He went away." He missed entering the kingdom, not because he was bad, but because he refused to make a committal of himself.

2. Not only is obedience the door into the kingdom, but it is the life of the kingdom. When the author of the book of Genesis undertakes to tell us what life meant to Enoch, he puts it in a single sentence: "Enoch walked with God." One day Enoch stretched a groping hand into the encircling gloom, and that almighty hand that is always feeling for yours and mine in the daylight and dark found the hand of Enoch, and he thus became acquainted with God. After he met God, nothing else seemed quite so worth while as to walk with him. But

how did this acquaintance ripen into friendship? The writer to the Hebrews answers that question: "He had this testimony, that he pleased God." That is, he walked with God through daily obedience.

So it was with Paul. When he first met Jesus, he surrendered to him. He died to his own will and to his own way. But that one death was not enough. Paul affirms, "I die daily." Every day he died afresh. He died to his own plans and purposes that he might make his own the plans and purposes of his Lord. It was this daily dying that enabled him to pass from the "these things" of his conversion to the "those things" of an ever-growing Christian experience.

3. "Father, I trust my spirit to thy hands." This is what the Bible means by perfection. If it is the least I can do and be a Christian, it is also the most I can do either in time or in eternity. In fact, if I do this, nothing else is required. This puts us all on an equal footing. There are a thousand things that you can do that I cannot. I can do some things that you cannot. But we can all do God's best. We can give ourselves to him. That is not only good, in the mind of our Lord; it is perfection.

IV

"Father, I trust my spirit to thy hands." Since this is all God asks of us, what ought we to do about it?

1. We ought to make full committal of ourselves in the here and now. We are to make this committal not because it is a small and easy matter. When Paul beseeches us to

76

present our bodies, our very selves, to God, he does not encourage us to do this because it will cost us nothing. On the contrary, it will cost us everything. We are to give in the faith that what we give he will accept. Let us therefore give ourselves to God with the assurance that he will gladly accept us.

2. Let us dedicate ourselves to God in the faith that what he accepts he remakes. I read of a great artist who was spending a few days in a humble home. It so happened that while he was a guest the little girl of the family had a birthday. Among the presents she received was a silk fan. It was a fairly ordinary affair, but when she showed it to the artist he said, "If you will let me keep this for a little while, I will paint you a picture on it."

But she snatched it away, saying, "You shan't spoil my fan."

If she had only trusted him, he would have given it back with its beauty and worth increased a thousandfold. Give yourself to God, and more and more he will transform you into the image of his glory.

3. Give yourself to God, and he will use you. He may not always use you in the way of your own choosing. He may not always lead you in green pastures beside still waters. He will not always use you in a fashion to make you comfortable. In using his own Son in the finest possible fashion he could not permit him to by-pass Calvary. As he uses you, you may become increasingly acquainted with the Cross. But use you he will.

4. Finally, if you give yourself to God, not only will

77

he accept, transform, and use you, but he will walk with you to the very end. I am quite sure that the Good Shepherd who has been with his sheep during the sunny days will not leave them at nightfall when they need him most. I have no slightest envy of the man who is master of his fate and captain of his soul. I have no desire to venture into life alone, nor do I dare face eternity alone. But if I pray with my Lord this prayer, "I trust my spirit to thy hands," I can face both today and tomorrow without fear.

Wm F Kuffeit -
Hugo Herman -
Mn Ovendahl -
Harry Kuffert -
Phil Heefner -
Cliff Lamb -
Karl Schlieman